CW00540449

MAKING WALKING STICKS FOR A HOBBY

MAKING
WALKING STICKS
FOR A HOBBY

David Dawson

ARTHUR H. STOCKWELL LTD.
Elms Court   Ilfracombe   Devon
Established 1898

British Library Cataloguing-in-Publication Data.
A catalogue record for this book is available
from the British Library.

Wrapper illustration courtesy of
Derbyshire Times Newspaper Group

ISBN 0 7223 3309-9
Printed in Great Britain by
Arthur H. Stockwell Ltd.
Elms Court   Ilfracombe
Devon

LIST OF ILLUSTRATIONS

CONTENTS

FOREWORD

The author has spent his working life in engineering. Firstly as an apprentice and finally as a Director with special responsibility for jig and tool design and manufacturing methods. Despite the fact that every working day involved dealing with steel and their alloys, etc., there was always an interest in working with wood and the enjoyment in working with woodcutting tools.

It was not surprising that, on retirement it seemed a natural progression to find a hobby using wood as a medium, and his thoughts turned to woodcarving. However, whilst searching the library bookshelves for books on this subject, several books on walking sticks and relating methods of manufacture captured his attention.

After much interesting reading it was obvious that the subject was far more involved and interesting, and time-consuming than the layman would have first envisaged. It was a subject which would involve design and many facets of the practical side of manufacture and production ideas.

The bait was taken and the decision to "have-a-go" materialised.

Walking in the countryside with his wife Audrey was always pleasurable, so collecting a few shanks whilst out walking resulted in the ideal combination of exercise and a hobby in the making.

Almost twelve months elapsed before several shanks, collected whilst out walking, were dry enough to be straightened. Two particular ones were selected out of about a dozen, to be the experimental ones.

The first one chosen was a very nicely marked hazel shank for Audrey; the second one being a heavier ash stick for his own use.

The straightening process took some time but eventually the shanks were ready for dressing. A well-seasoned piece of sycamore provided sufficient material for two heads which were dowelled and glued, and once tips had been fitted, both sticks were treated with two coats of yacht varnish. *(Refer to front cover here.)*

9

My first sticks

Both sticks are in regular use still, and are adorned with many badges depicting places of interest visited over the past few years.

The author has to date made well over fifty sticks of all shapes and sizes. Many have been given to relatives and friends who enjoy walking with a well-made comfortable stick as an aid.

This book is written with the intention of providing encouragement and 'know-how' to similarly-minded people who wish to start a creative and interesting hobby.

Stick-dressing is a hobby which is ideally suitable for retired people, who maybe having time to spare, require a hobby which will help fill in this time, but at the same time, requiring minimum financial outlay.

INTRODUCTION

The walking stick has been man's aid for hundreds of years. The common stick or staff has been used for fighting and have often been disguised to serve as swords or pistols. The latter ones of course are now outlawed, but still exists in many collections.

Old one-piece sticks

In the latter part of the 19th century and into the earlier part of the 20th century, the cane was very popular as a 'fashion' aid for city gentlemen of that era.

My father had such a cane with a silver mount of intricate shape on the end of the handle. This particular cane is illustrated together with other old sticks in the photograph on the left.

Commercially produced sticks are generally one-piece items, usually made in ash and steam-bent. The steam-bending is a simple operation and certainly a low-cost procedure, especially when carried out in large quantities. They are the cheapest form of stick to be purchased.

However, for a hobby the stick-maker should preferably not spend his time on this type of stick but endeavour to produce a better class of stick worthy of the time spent producing it

11

and at the same time increasing his enjoyment through achieving a more sophisticated design of stick, and pleasure in its use.

Several books have been written by stick-dressers who have practised the art most of their lives, and due to their professionalism have entered stick-dressers' competitions such as those held at The Great Yorkshire Show at Harrowgate, and at other popular craft fairs, etc. The professional stick-dresser will be skilled at producing all kinds of sticks.

He will produce both single-piece and two-piece sticks, not only in wood but will use horn of several varieties on both walking stick heads and for shepherds' crooks and thumb-sticks. Many of these stick-dressers judge competitions in addition to writing books on the subject.

This book will concentrate on walking sticks using only natural woods for both the shank and the head, although some of the photographic illustrations depict one-piece items and attempts to describe their disadvantages.

Stick-dressing was very popular with the shepherds and gamekeepers of a hundred years ago who were employed on large isolated farms of that era. Quite often they lived in tied cottages on the farmland many miles from populated areas and with time on their hands needed some form of relaxing pastime. They usually had ample supplies of horn, and would make beautifully carved heads using only basic tools, one being a good sharp pocketknife.

Quite often they seasoned their shanks suspended in bundles from the rafters of a barn or a hayloft, and although the slow drying was an advantage in as much that splitting was duly avoided, they would wait probably two years before work could proceed.

The only heat that was available to the shepherd in his cottage in those days would be an oil lamp, so the straightening process would be also a very lengthy operation.

Stick-dressing today is not quite so arduous due to the availability of modern tools and heating facilities. It is not surprising therefore that even the novice of today can produce a well-balanced, good-looking stick more easily than his counterpart of 100 years ago.

Hopefully this book will be a useful guide to many people, who like myself, require a hobby which is totally satisfying and combines walking in the countryside with the practical side of working with wood as seen there.

STICK COLLECTING (SHANKS) AND TOOLS

The following three photographs show typical hedgerows where suitable shanks may be found, but it is most important to remember that permission must be sought from the landowner before cutting any sticks.

Ideal stick sources

The search for sticks suitable for seasoning and subsequently straightening, can sometimes be tedious but success at this stage, so early in the stick-dressing procedure, can be very rewarding if the right type of stick can be found.

Look for sticks that are reasonably straight; this will reduce the work content later on. Slight bends in one direction are acceptable but avoid collecting sticks which have dogleg bends, if at all possible. Straightening these can be most difficult and time-consuming.

Ideally the best time of the year to go stick gathering is late autumn and onwards, when the sap is receding. This will speed up the seasoning (drying out) time which can be anything from six months to one year, depending on the type of wood to be seasoned and what type of drying facilities are available.

Initially the novice should be satisfied with a bundle of one dozen sticks. This will be quite sufficient with which to start up his hobby. Cut the sticks about three feet to three feet six inches long and about three-quarter inch to one inch thick maximum at the thickest end. Trim off any side shoots and tie them up firmly into two bundles of six to a bundle.

Bundling your sticks

15

A small saw with coarse pitched teeth as shown in the following photograph is most suitable. An ideal type, which is easy and safe to carry about, has a separate handle and quick-change replacement blades. Together with a sharp pocketknife these are, at this stage, all the tools one needs.

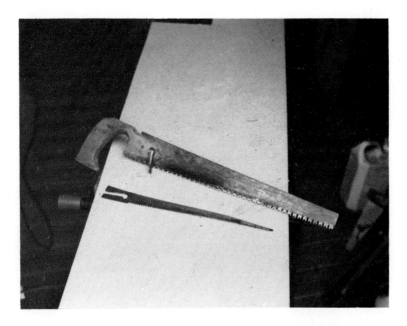

Stick-cutting saw

MATERIALS

The choice of materials used in stick-dressing is so variable it can be suggested that the newcomer to the hobby restricts his choice to the well-tried favourites such as, ash, holly and hazel. Another fine wood for shanks, which I have used with great success, is privet.

Unfortunately it is most unusual to find privet growing high enough to cut suitable thickness shanks of acceptable length for stick-dressing but if you are fortunate to find a very old hedge, which has been allowed to grow without ever being trimmed down, then seek permission to be allowed to cut a few lengths.

Ash. This is most suitable for shanks and is used regularly in the manufacture of mass-produced walking sticks. They are the steam-bent one-piece variety. However a good ash sapling can still be used as a shank, and when seasoned and straightened, can be an ideal candidate for dressing with a separate head.

Holly. I have found holly to be an excellent wood for the novice stick-dresser. Usually, almost straight examples can be found growing in hedges. So many holly bushes have suckers growing low down, often vertical and straight, ideal for shanks. My experience has shown holly to take a little longer than other woods to dry out, but once seasoned and straightened where necessary, it makes an ideal stick and takes a polish exceedingly well.

Some stick-dressers prefer to peel the bark from holly shanks but I have found out that by seasoning them slowly, the bark will stay intact without cracking or splitting. A very fine sandpapering, and two coats of yacht varnish, gives an excellent, almost black result. The knots will stay almost white, providing a handsome contrast.

Hazel. This wood is ideal for shanks and is a favourite of the majority of stick-dressers, not only due to its often natural straightness, but because of its excellent, almost artistic-like mottled finish on the bark. Hazel was in use commercially many years ago when thatching was so popular. The thatcher would cut lengths of coppice-grown hazel from which to fashion pegs to assist in holding down the thatch. Stick-hunters of today should look out for these abandoned coppices and also for wild hazels on hedgerows and on edges of woodland. Once again it is important that one gets permission from the owner before cutting any shanks from these areas.

Oak. This is not commonly used for shanks by stick-dressers; one reason being due to the dogleg type of growth and the resulting difficulties in the straightening process.

If you are fortunate enough to find an oak tree which has recently been pollarded then quite often, straight vertical growth can be cut for shanks, with rewarding results.

I have made two sticks in oak from a pollarded tree and although it took extra time to season and the straightening problems were more than usual, the resulting shanks were very strong, and eventually two very handsome sticks were produced.

The bark was unattractive but I peeled it in such a way that a portion of the under-bark stayed intact and the result was a 'seaside-rock' stripe effect. Several coats of yacht varnish were applied to both the shank and the beech head, which combined well together.

Elder. Make sure you do not use young elder due to the centre being soft. The central pithy area makes it too weak to use for sticks. Older growth is fine and can be used with or without peeling. It has great strength making it ideal for walking sticks. If you prefer peeled sticks, then elder gives a very attractive finish due to its yellow tinge and irregular pattern and grooving. Do not peel until it is fully dried out (seasoned).

Earlier in this particular heading of materials, I advised the novice to adhere to the three most popular woods for shanks but of course once one has tried these and wishes to experiment, then 'elder' is fine.

Broom. This is another of the slightly unusual woods which will produce a fine walking stick shank, although maybe too lightweight for some people. However, whilst some stick-makers prefer to peel the bark from broom, I prefer to leave the bark intact, since it can display an unusual pattern of prominent slightly raised ovalised areas.

Gorse. I have found this wood rather difficult to straighten but it can be used to make a fine walking stick shank. It grows in abundance on roadsides and on patches of common land which is noticeably no use for any other form of cultivation. The bark is totally unattractive and it is advisable to peel the shank to expose the unusual grain, and together with the natural twist and gnarled appearance, the extra effort in working this wood, is well worthwhile.

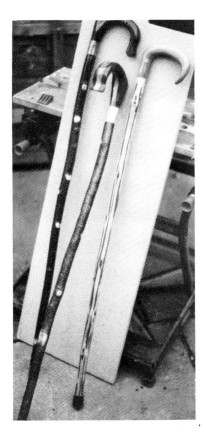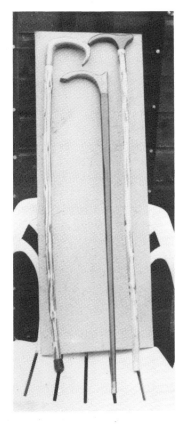

Decorated sticks

19

SEASONING (DRYING OUT)

Seasoning is the correct term used for the "drying-out" process. Very little can be written about this subject except to say one has to be very patient since it is a slow process and one cannot see any visual changes in the sticks during the drying out stage.

However, personal experience shows that once you have an adequate supply of shanks — this could be two bundles of six shanks in each bundle — firmly tied together, then they should be placed vertically in a damp-free, airy spot. A fuel store or garden shed is ideal. This initial stage of the drying out will be about three to four months.

As previously described, the shepherd of days gone by used a hayloft or similar place to hang up bundles of sticks and would wait probably two years or more before he would make any attempt to begin the straightening process.

Today most of us now have some form of central heating, so we can use an area near the boiler for the final stage of drying out the shanks. My own experience has shown, once the initial stage is over, the bundles can be placed preferably vertical, about nine inches to twelve inches away from the boiler itself and anything from four to six months is ample for all the woods I have used.

On no account should the seasoning process be speeded up; to do so can only lead to splitting and cracking, and all the work put in to gathering the sticks will have been to no avail. Should you prefer to peel the sticks eventually, this should be done after the complete drying out stage is complete. Leaving the bark intact at this time, will help to prevent cracking and splitting.

Many years ago I enjoyed wood turning. I built a simple headstock which was ideal for bowl-turning. I was fortunate to be given a large piece of "yew" which, although not freshly cut, was still not yet ready for being worked.

I made enquiries about a water-soluble wax treatment called

P.E.G. — this is Polyethylene Glycol and is very expensive. However in the end I did not use it because it limits the type of finish the finished article will take, even though it does speed up the drying process by forcing out the water in the wood and replaces it with wax. If you envisage treating your sticks with any type of varnish, then you will be advised not to contemplate using P.E.G.

STRAIGHTENING

No matter how careful and methodical you are when searching for suitable shanks, a perfectly straight one is rarely found, and so even with the best shanks, an element of straightening will be necessary.

A word of warning here and it must be stressed that unless you have dried out your sticks perfectly, then the work involved in the straightening process will have been a waste of time and effort. Green sticks will return to their bent condition within a short period and your finished walking stick will be useless.

A further bit of advice is, never use a naked flame on the shank being straightened. The shepherd of years gone by had no modern hot air accessory, so an oil lamp or similar heat source was his only answer. Some form of protection such as aluminium foil is used nowadays to protect the bark from being scorched.

Over the past few years, I have only had a couple of shanks that were straight enough, after the seasoning process, to be used for dressing with a separate head without any form of straightening.

There are numerous ways one can straighten shanks, but in my experience, there are only two types of heat source. Steam can be used most effectively using an electric kettle with a continuous boiling and steaming system without switching itself off until it boils dry! Placed between a suitable rack, the shank mounted above the steam, the bend can be taken out in stages.

However, I have found the ideal heat source is a Black & Decker hot air gun — the kind used for paint stripping, and together with a form of holding the shank straight, the operation is quite simple. It can be time-consuming because most sticks will be bent in more than one place, so the clamping and heating of each bend alternately, has to be carried out.

A good work bench is a simple form of clamping and wedges between the overhanging ends of the shank and the bench can be

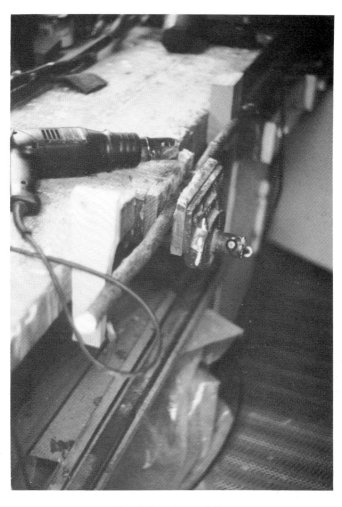

Straightening sticks

used to force the bent area into a straighter line. Whilst in this situation the heat gun must be used to apply heat to the bent area. An alternative method is to use two pieces of straight timber, about three inches by two inches section, and clamp the shank between them. Use the heat gun as previously described, traversing along the stick slowly with the nozzle about two inches distance from the shank.

Straightening sticks

The ideal piece of equipment to be used for the straightening process, along with the warm air gun, is the Black & Decker "workmate". Great care should be taken not to burn the shank. Keeping the nozzle about two inches from the shank, and a steady backwards and forwards movement along the shank, is all that is required.

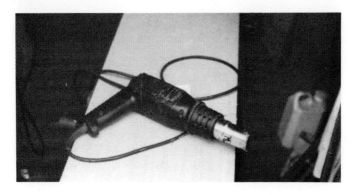

Heat gun

When the shank is clamped in the "workmate", there is the added facility of being able to heat the shank on the underside, which should be done at three or four minute intervals. To fully straighten a bent shank, these operations will have to be repeated several times, moving the stick along as each bend is worked upon.

Each session of heating should allow about two hour intervals. Once you feel satisfied that the shank has had sufficient treatment, then it should be left in the clamped position until the following day. On release of the loaded clamps, it will be easily seen whether the straightening process has been 100% successful. I have found that this is rarely the case and the operation has to be repeated until a fully straight shank has been achieved.

Heat gun in use

ONE-PIECE STICKS

Personally I find a great deal of satisfaction can be achieved by producing a two-piece stick, because a great deal of variation can be brought about in the design of the finished stick by fitting an artistically-shaped head, either by shape or by the type of wood used.

However there is always a place for the one-piece stick, and although the commercially produced ones are nearly all steam-bent, it doesn't rule out the naturally produced ones.

Nature quite often produces its own odd shapes and the accompanying photographs illustrate some examples. The handles

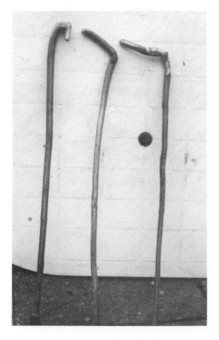

Natural one-piece sticks

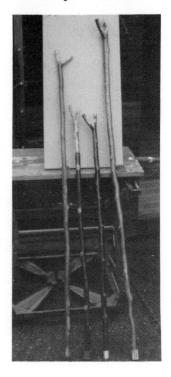

formed by nature can look quite unusual and create interesting conversation, but it is rare to find nature creating a handle that can match the comfort of a well-made head designed specifically to suit one's hand.

Steam-bent sticks

However thumb-sticks remain very popular amongst ramblers and if you find a stick with a well-shaped 'Y' and is long enough to create a thumb-stick, then cut it at that length. It would be a shame to cut it down to walking stick length.

The other one-piece stick which I do like very much, is the knob-stick. These can be made easily if you are fortunate, when stick hunting, to find a straight stick growing from a heavier branch, which if cut about three inches either side of the junction, will provide ample material to form the knob. I suggest three inches either side to give a six-inch piece 'T' section, since during the drying out, cracking could occur in the thicker section. Leaving extra material will enable the cracked ends to be cut off, still leaving sufficient to form the knob.

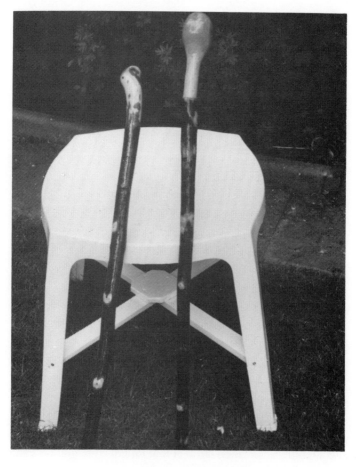

Natural one-piece sticks

Quite often the one-piece steam-bent stick will try to revert to its original straightness if left out in the rain, or perhaps left in the sun on the rear parcel shelf of the car.

A simple form of jig, which I have used to great effect, is shown in the accompanying illustration. A few minutes' careful heating to the head, using a hot air gun, and a slow tightening of the clamping screws, can, if you are patient and keep alternating the heating and tightening procedure, give you a reformed bent head.

Bending jig

HANDLES (HEADS)

The design of a head can stretch one's imagination and stick-dressers who enter competitions often carve birds and fish, etc., in wood or horn, to decorate their walking stick heads. A popular decoration on a Scottish competitor's stick head, would be a thistle.

However, this type of enhancement may be a little too advanced for the novice stick-dresser, but something to aim at in the future!

Let us be satisfied at this stage by making heads in wood, especially as horn is very expensive, and for most people difficult to obtain.

Solid hardwood of several varieties can be used for heads. The most popular choice being beech, elm, mahogany and oak. My first sticks had sycamore heads, for the only reason that I happened to have a nice well seasoned piece about one and a quarter inches thick, large enough to cut out two nice shaped heads. *(See front cover.)*

Whereas natural wood is available for the shanks and a few stick-collecting trips can bring in an ample supply, then wood for heads is not so easily come by. Small pieces of

My first sticks

hardwood for your heads can be found at some wood yards, and if you know of a local furniture manufacturer or cabinet-maker, then these are likely sources of scrap-ends of hardwood.

Some time ago, I salvaged an old oak sideboard which yielded some fine pieces of oak for heads. The drawer fronts were about three-quarters of an inch thick and the top board about seven-eights of an inch thick, which is just about the minimum thickness one should start with.

I have made some very attractive heads from mahogany, which is normally very difficult to find as scrap-ends. However, recently we had double glazing fitted and when the old window frames were removed, I noticed the windowsills were solid mahogany. Plenty of sawing down and planing kept me going in heads for sometime. I now watch for double glazing teams in the area and make a point of begging the windowsills before they go in the skip!

Quite often the hardwood which comes into your possession, for example the oak linings of drawers, is not thick enough to make a head. One solution to this problem is to clamp and glue

Joining materials for heads

31

two thicknesses together under pressure in a vice or between clamps. An attractive head can be made by using three thicknesses of timber; say one oak in the centre, sandwiched between two thicknesses of a contrasting timber such as mahogany.

Similarly, two pieces of timber can be glued and clamped together along their edges, where the thickness is suitable, but the width is insufficient to give you a good head.

Joining materials for heads

In all cases as above, the surfaces or edges to be glued, must be flat and clean before being clamped together. Clamps to be left for around twenty-four hours.

The design of the head depends on personal choice but in order not to waste time and timber, it is advisable to sketch your required shape on a piece of paper or thin cardboard. Once you have a shape drawn to your liking, cut it out. This template can be placed on your timber, and following a pencilled outline, cutting to shape can be commenced.

The ideal tool for cutting out the head to rough outline, is an electric jigsaw, but of course a bowsaw or fret saw can be used, or any saw capable of following a curved profile.

Cutting the heads

An alternative to sawing out the shape of the head, is to drill a series of holes around the pencilled outline, close enough to allow the waste to come away, and then using a coarse rasp, the rough shape of the head can be completed.

C

Cutting the heads

Once you have established a system of cutting out your heads, a few shapes should be taken to the rough outline. Quite some time is needed to produce a selection of heads, and this work can ideally be carried out during the period that your shanks are drying out.

The following two photographs show some heads I have roughly sawn to shape, including a few using the sandwich technique, and also one or two from laminated plywoods, which when finished can look very attractive. Their strength, due to being laminated, is several times stronger than a one-piece head.

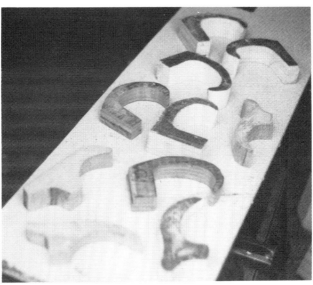

Selection of heads

These two photographs show clearly the effect of two contrasting timbers, when fitted to a shank and finally finished with two coats of yacht varnish.

Assorted sticks

The first photograph on the next page shows a display of files and rasps which are needed to assist in the rough shaping of the head. The cutter shown in the brace is called a hole-saw and is an ideal tool for shaping the thumb rest in the thumb-sticks.

The second photograph shows a Black & Decker electric file. This tool is beyond doubt the finest piece of equipment for the enthusiastic stick-dresser. Using varying grades of emery belt, the shaping of the head is simplified, and the speed material can be removed, is remarkable. Of course it is not an essential requirement for the beginner but once the hobby takes over, then you will find the electric file to be your best friend!

Of course, whatever method is used for semi-shaping the head, be it rasps, or files, etc., the final operation has to be hand sanding. Patience here is so important. A fine hazel shank can be spoilt when fitted to a poorly finished head. When sandpapering, always use two or three grades of paper, finishing with a very fine grade, before final varnishing.

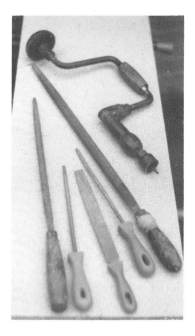

Tools

Electric file

SHANKING (STICKS)

This operation is the coming together of all the work done up to this point in time. The shanks have been drying for many months and heads have been cut, and roughly shaped in the meantime. The next step is to 'marry' together a head to a shank. Choose a heavy head for the thickest shank and subsequently the thinnest sticks for a lighter designed head. Also at this point be concerned with matching wood to wood. For example an oak head, which is light in colour, may look finer on a holly shank, which will be almost black when varnished. A little thought on this point can be well worthwhile.

Once you have decided on a choice of head and a mating shank, then the drilling, dowelling and gluing together can proceed.

Sometimes I have roughly shaped part of the head at this stage, but left the area where the head is to be drilled. This area is best left until the head is fitted to the shank, so a neat blend can be achieved at the joint.

Fitting a head, which is roughly shaped onto a shank, using the dowel but not yet glued, can help you in imagining what the finished stick will look like before gluing takes place. Experience here will help you decide.

A selection of dowels are shown in the following photograph. Generally speaking a hardwood dowel ten millimetres diameter, about four inches long is suitable. Screwed plastic or steel rod of the same proportions can be used and all these items can be purchased from local DIY stores.

Firstly make sure the face of the head and the end of the shank, where they will come together, are flat and true. This is most important since the more perfect the joint is, then the stronger the joint will be.

Drill the shank and the head ten millimetres diameter. The depth of the hole in each part to be two and an eighth inches to suit a dowel four inches long. A shorter dowel may be used if the shape of the chosen head restricts a two and an eighth inches deep hole being drilled. Adjust the dowel length accordingly but I suggest it should be no shorter than three inches.

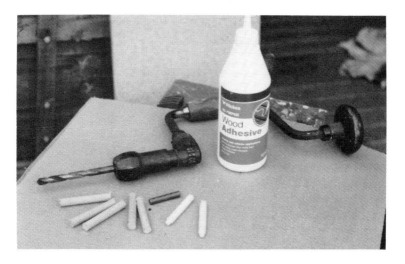

Selection of dowels

Providing the holes you drill are true in both the head and the shank, then when the dowel is inserted and the two parts pressed together, a good 'thin-line' joint should be achieved. Dress the faces until this is achieved before final gluing.

The gluing itself is a very important step in the shanking process. It is quite easy to make the error of only partially gluing the surface of the dowel, unless the following method is used, and the following three photographs attempt to illustrate this.

Firstly, using a commercially used wood glue, insert into the ten millimetre diameter hole in the head, about half a teaspoonful whilst in the upright position. Next, push the four inch long dowel into the hole until the glue emerges up the hole and around the dowel. Doing this guarantees the dowel is glued over its full length and around its diameter completely. Holding the shank vertically, repeat the operation of pouring half a teaspoonful into the ten millimetre diameter hole, then lower the glued shank over the upright dowel in the head.

Joining head to shank

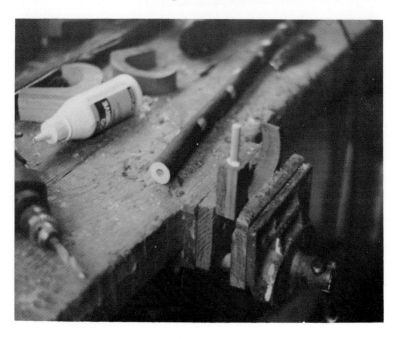

Excess glue will cover the area of the joint as the shank is pressed down on the head. Glue will as previously described, fully glue the dowel into the shank. Exert a little pressure to bring the shank down onto the head and wipe the surplus glue from the joint, and with a final inspection of the accuracy of the joint, the two items can be left to 'set' completely for twenty-four hours before any further work is contemplated.

When a twenty-four hour period has elapsed, the glue should have cured and this is an ideal time to cut the stick to its finished length and fit a tip. The measurement for the overall length of a walking stick varies obviously from person to person. A rule of thumb length can be from the ground up to the wrist joint.

Joining head to shank

41

Assorted sticks

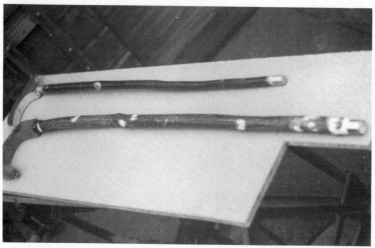

TIPPING AND FERRULING

All sticks should be tipped to prevent wear and tear from contact on the ground. For those people requiring a nonslip tip, then rubber tips of varying sizes and shapes are easily available from sports shops, craft supply outlets, and from outdoor pursuit equipment stockists.

Tapered brass and steel tips can also be purchased and to this end a taper should be filed on the end of the shank. The tip should be a tap-on fit. For added retention it can be glued or secured by a small tack through into the shank. All to be done after ensuring the overall length of the walking stick has been measured correctly.

Tipping

On many occasions, I have resorted to using a much cheaper method of tipping by utilising odd bits of piping; either, steel, aluminium or copper. The local plumber will oblige you with his useless cutoffs, and electricians' conduit is also a very useful and easily obtainable substitute.

The above photograph shows the end of the shank being prepared for tipping with a parallel piece of steel conduit. Here again it is essential that it be a good tight fit. It can of course be glued or retained with a tack through into the stick if preferred as added security. I advise a piece of conduit about one and a half inches long and after being knocked into place on the shank, it can be cut off neatly about one and a quarter inches long sawing through the tip and the shank at the same time. This should guarantee a tidy flush fit to the end of the shank.

The advantage of fitting a metal tip to the walking stick is twofold, in as much that it does prevent wear and tear initially, but it leaves open the option to add a rubber tip also if, and when it may be needed for a nonslip situation.

The photograph displaying a selection of tips shows some copper examples too. The larger copper ones are ideal for using as ferrules, fitted between the head and the shank. A polished copper or brass ferrule can make a walking stick quite attractive in addition to serving a dual purpose in that it strengthens the area where the shank has been drilled for the dowel.

Tipping

The operation of fitting a ferrule has to be done obviously before the head is fitted to the shank. I prefer to fit a ferrule before I drill the shank and it is done in exactly the same way as fitting a tip; that is by reducing the end of the shank at the thickest end so that the ferrule is a tap-on fit and finishes flush with the end of the shank.

Tipping

In both cases of tipping and ferruling, some form of adhesive can be used to increase the strength of the fit.

FINISHING THE HEAD (HANDLE)

Once the head is glued firmly to the shank using your particular choice of dowel and twenty-four hours has elapsed since the gluing was done, then work can commence on finish-shaping the head.

As previously described, a selection of rasps and files are needed. Preparatory work can be carried out with a good sharp pocketknife to roughly remove some bulky excess wood.

The finished shape of the head depends entirely on the stick-maker's requirements, but an overall curvaceous form should be aimed at. Obviously there must be no sharp corners or edges, and the overall finish should be smooth to the touch.

The photographs below, show the author using strip abrasive cloth to obtain a good smooth rounded face to the inside of the

Finish sanding the heads

head. This method of using a narrow abrasive strip pulling backwards and forwards, gives an excellent form, which is necessary for the user's hand to grip comfortably.

Finish sanding the heads

An assortment of different heads are shown below, together with one or two ideas of simple adornment by peeling the bark below the head or forming rings by removing narrow strips of bark.

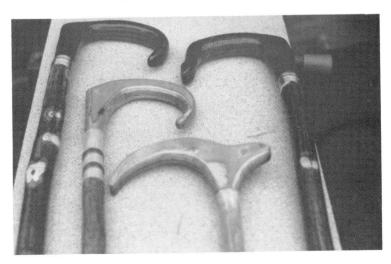

Assorted heads

STICK DESIGN VARIATIONS

Generally speaking, stick-dressers use saplings and branches from natural growth resources and the majority of my walking sticks have followed this method; always assuming it is the most natural and oldest established method.

However, I have been tempted on occasions to stray away from 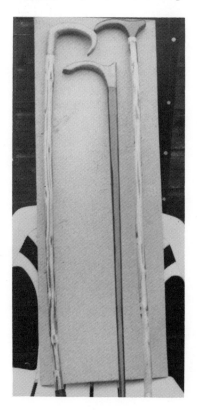 the accepted usage of 'growing' wood and have on many occasions used mahogany, oak and beech, sawn from bulk seasoned timber, to produce a selection of walking sticks. The design of these sticks could be described as gentlemen's 'town' sticks. It could be said that they are the modern version of the 'cane', except that they are much stiffer and stronger and are ideal for anyone who relies on their stick to give them maximum support at all times.

The photograph on the left illustrates three sticks in oak with heads in beech, elm and mahogany. All three sticks are noticeably different due to the different heads, showing clearly that when bringing heads and shanks together at gluing stage, it is important to try to envisage what the final stick will look like. I try to have a contrasting

Decorated sticks

48

colour wood, and sometimes shape, when matching head to shank.

In this photograph, two of the oak sticks have a striped effect. This has been achieved by peeling the whole of the top outer bark, but by careful scraping only partially the under-bark, before sanding smooth and varnishing. The stick in the centre is also of oak but not from a tree branch. This stick is from an oak plank from an old piece of furniture, tapered and shaped to an oval section. The stick was finish-tipped with copper. The completed stick was most attractive, and quite easily made, and of course needed no seasoning or straightening!

The next two photographs show samples of mahogany and teak sticks. They are, in general, tapered and are of square or rectangular section, with champered corners. When fitted with a copper or brass ferrule, they look extremely handsome. The heads are noticeably different in shape to a crook type head, giving them a more distinguished look for their particular use.

"Town" sticks

49

Plain-headed sticks

I have mentioned on one or two occasions how I keep a sharp lookout for any sort of hardwood from which to cut heads, but this also applies to old seasoned hardwood which may be suitable for shanks. The following photograph shows part of a mahogany windowsill, a sideboard leg and a length of beech (its former use unknown). These three examples are ideal candidates for cutting lengthwise, and shaping to one's own requirements, and when fitted with a good head, will make fine walking sticks.

Alternative hardwood for sticks

In my introduction, I suggested that the novice requiring to make stick-dressing a hobby, would probably be wasting a lot of his time and effort making one-piece sticks with a steam-bent head. My suggestion is based purely due to the fact that commercially made sticks of this type, are plentiful, and being cheap to produce in large quantities, their retail price relates to this fact.

However, one cannot ignore the beauty and 'feel' of a very old walking stick and the next photograph shows three such sticks.

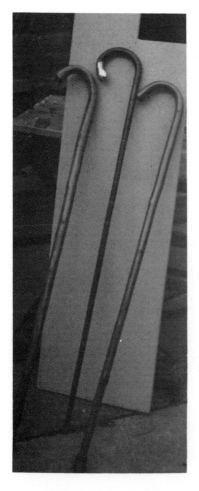

They are all very old and the smoothness and patina of the wood depicts their life span. The cane in the centre of the photograph belonged to my father and I believe it was a present from his father on the occasion of his twenty-first birthday — together with a straw boater! In his day the cane and boater would be part of a gentleman's Sunday outfit. The silver knob gives the cane a character of its own and was typical of the type of ornamentation of the earlier 1900s. This cane is now a family heirloom and hopefully will remain so for many more years to come.

Hopefully the novice stick-maker will take heed of these suggested innovative ideas and remembers that *'design'* is as important to the finished product as is practical perfection.

Old one-piece sticks

MODERN TOOLS

Very little expense is necessary to start the novice off with a stick-making hobby, but of course all practical hobbies entailing the manufacture of an item, will require some tools in one form or another.

Firstly, the inexpensive tools are generally hand tools and it is necessary to have a couple of rasps, a file or two, and a simple coarse-tooth saw. A foldaway pruning saw is ideal, or as previously illustrated, a loose-bladed handsaw where blades are interchangeable and range from very coarse to fine teeth.

A hand drill or brace and a ten millimetre bit will be suitable for drilling the dowel holes, but of course an electric drill is much more suitable and is often the one electric tool most DIY handymen possess. A stout pocketknife and various grades of sandpaper just about completes the list of requirements; plus some varnish of course.

Once the bug bites, the beginner will no doubt feel the hobby is worth further investment in tools, etc., to make the work a little easier, and of course efficiency results in a finer product all round. The list of more expensive tools is not endless however and the photograph on the left shows the Black & Decker workmate with a hot air blowgun, an electric file and of course the electric drill.

As soon as the novice

Electic tools

53

takes possession of the more modern tools, he will speed up several processes and enjoy the hobby all the more.

The result obtained from the use of these pieces of equipment, enables the stick-maker to increase production and build in design ideas so that eventually, like myself, he will have supplied many relatives and friends with fine walking sticks and then will be pondering how to dispose of excess sticks.

Will pleasure turn to profit? Selling sticks is not an easy decision to make and still harder is where to sell them. Ideally a small retail outlet willing to buy the sticks on the spot is the answer. Otherwise it can be a case of supplying a number of sticks on a 'sale-or-return' basis. I have not tried selling my sticks at a craft fair but this I suppose would suit some stick-makers and would certainly bring in the social contact. I have been to many craft fairs and have not seen one stall showing sticks so, who knows this may be a good investment.

Do remember when selling your sticks, wherever your outlet may be, do ask a fair price so that your efforts are rewarded.

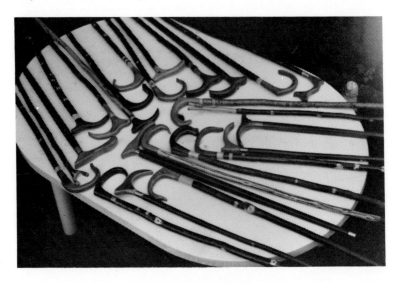

Stick collection

Whoever reads this book, I do hope it helps to bring stick-dressing into your life. The very best of luck in this hobby.